A Mob of
Kangaroos

Heinemann Library
Chicago, Illinois

Richard and Louise Spilsbury

Originated by Dot Gradations Ltd
Printed in Hong Kong, China by Wing King Tong

08 07 06 05 04
10 9 8 7 6 5 4 3 2 1

Library of Congress Cataloging-in-Publication Data
Spilsbury, Louise.
  A mob of kangaroos / Louise and Richard Spilsbury.
    p. cm. -- (Animal groups) (Dk readers)
Summary: Describes the physical characteristics, behavior, habitat, and
group life of kangaroos.
Includes bibliographical references and index.
  ISBN 1-4034-4690-3 (HC lib. bdg.) 1-4034-5417-5 (PB)
  1. Kangaroos--Juvenile literature. [1. Kangaroos.] I. Spilsbury,
Richard, 1963- II. Title. III. Series. IV. Dorling Kindersley readers.
  QL737.M35S65 2004
  599.2'22--dc21
                                2003010350

Acknowledgments
The author and publishers are grateful to the following for permission to reproduce copyright material:

p. 4 Ardea/Jean paul Ferrero; pp. 5, 25, 26 NPL/Dave Watts; p. 6 OSF/Des & Jan Barlett; p. 8 Theo Allofs; pp. 9, 12 Ardea/John Cancalosi; p. 10 PA/A.N.T; p. 11 NHPA/Gerard Lacz; p. 11 OSF/Tony Bomford; p. 13 OSF/Hans & Judy Beste/AA; pp. 14, 18, 21, 23 NHPA/Martin Harvey; p. 15 TRIP/Australian Picture Library; p. 16 OSF/Alan Root; p. 17 FLPA/Minden Pictures; p. 19 OSF/Adrienne T. Gibson; p. 20 OSF/Stan Osolinski; p. 21 Ardea/P. Morris; p. 22 Corbis/Theo Allofs; p. 24 TRIP/Eric Smith; p. 27 Corbis/Paul A. Souders; p. 28 Still Pictures.

Cover photograph of a kangaroo mob, reproduced with permission of FLPA/Gerard Lacz.

Every effort has been made to contact copyright holders of any material reproduced in this book. Any omissions will be rectified in subsequent printings if notice is given to the publisher.

Contents

Some words are shown in bold, **like this.** You can find out what they mean by looking in the glossary.

What Are Kangaroos?

Kangaroos are the only large **mammals** in the world that hop to get around. They have short front legs that they use when walking, but if kangaroos want to move quickly, they hop on their large and powerful back legs. Using this bouncing run, the fastest kangaroos can travel up to 31 miles (50 kilometers) an hour and leap 26 feet (8 meters) in each jump!

This is a red kangaroo. Kangaroos have small heads and large ears. Their big feet and large tails help them balance when they run.

What are marsupials?

Kangaroos belong to a special group of mammals called **marsupials**. All marsupials give birth to young that are only partly developed. The young finish developing in a pouch on the front of their mother's belly, instead of growing inside their mother like most mammals.

4

Kinds of kangaroo

There are about 56 **species** of kangaroo in the world. They range in size from the tiny musky rat kangaroos that averages about 15 inches (37 centimeters) in length to 7-foot (2-meter) tall red kangaroos. There are six large species known as kangaroos and wallaroos. The smaller species are rat kangaroos, potoroos, tree kangaroos, pademelons, and wallabies.

All kangaroos have coats of short hair that range in color from white to gray and from tan to red. In all species the adult **males** are much bigger than the **females** and have more **muscular** chests and arms. Red and grey female kangaroos are known as **flyers**, large males are called **boomers**, and young kangaroos are **joeys**.

The musky rat kangaroo is the smallest of all kangaroos. It only weighs about 1 pound (500 grams) and is similar in size to a large guinea pig.

Do kangaroos live in groups?

Some **species** of kangaroos spend most of their time alone. They only join other adults to **mate.** Others are more **social** animals. This means that for much of the time they live, feed, and stay together in groups and make friendships that last a lifetime. Groups of kangaroos are called mobs.

Red and gray kangaroos

In this book we look mainly at the two largest species of kangaroo—the red kangaroo and the gray kangaroo. Red kangaroos get their name from the **males'** rust-colored coat, even though the **females** have blue-gray hair. Gray kangaroos are gray with white undersides.

This is a group of gray kangaroos. Individual red and gray kangaroos spend some time alone, but most of their lives are spent as part of a group called a mob.

What Is a Kangaroo Mob?

Kangaroo mobs have between 2 and 30 members. In a small mob there may be just one adult male, two or three females with **joeys**, and two or three young males. Members of the mob wander off alone or with a few others so you rarely see the whole mob together at the same time. Sometimes several mobs gather together in large groups, especially when food is scarce, such as in times of **drought**.

Living in a mob

One of the advantages of living in a mob is that some kangaroos can act as lookouts while others feed or relax. Kangaroos are especially careful when going for a drink at a **watering hole**. While a mob drinks, there is always one or more guards on duty, keeping a careful eye out for **predators**.

What is a kangaroo's day like?

In warmer months, the kangaroos in a mob usually spend most of the day resting in a shady spot. At night, when it is cooler, they search large areas for food. In cooler months, kangaroos also may feed in the middle of the day, and on warm afternoons they may sunbathe.

This is a mob of gray kangaroos in Murramarang National Park, New South Wales, Australia.

Who's who in a mob?

The leader of a mob of kangaroos is the strongest and usually the largest **male** in the group. He is called the **dominant** kangaroo. He is usually the only male who **mates** with the **female** kangaroos in the mob. This means that he is the father of all the **joeys** in the group. As the dominant kangaroo, he also gets the best feeding spots and the shadiest resting places.

The other male kangaroos in the mob are ranked in importance based on their size, so the smallest male is the least important. The older females are dominant over the younger ones. These older females may lead the mob to good places to feed or rest.

This big red kangaroo is known as an old boomer, or old man—the leader of his mob.

Where Do Kangaroos Live?

Almost all the different **species** of kangaroo live in Australia, but a few live in New Guinea and other islands nearby. The gray kangaroo is the only kind of kangaroo that lives on the island of Tasmania.

Different kinds of kangaroo live in different kinds of **habitats.** Some species live only in **deserts** and open **grassland.** Some live on dry rocky hillsides, while others live in forests. Gray kangaroos live in a wide variety of habitats, from high mountain forests to dry open spaces. The red kangaroo lives in Australia's grasslands, **scrublands**—also called the **bush**—and hot deserts.

What is a tree kangaroo?

Tree kangaroos live, as their name suggests, in trees. They have longer front legs, are better at walking, and have longer, curved claws than other kangaroos. These help them climb and live in trees.

Many kangaroos live on dry open lands in northern Australia.

What is a home range?

A **home range** is the area an animal or group of animals travels around to feed, care for young, and rest. Most kangaroo mobs roam over a range several miles (a few kilometers) across. The home ranges of different mobs of kangaroos often overlap, but mobs do not try to keep each other out. Kangaroos like to stay inside their home range. If they are forced to move away to find food, perhaps during a **drought**, they usually return later.

Rock wallabies are small kangaroos that live in groups on steep rocky hillsides.

Tree kangaroos live in parts of the rainforests of northeast Australia and New Guinea.

How do kangaroos deal with the heat?

Most red and gray kangaroos live in **habitats** that are extremely hot and dry. They live in areas of land where the weather is too hot and dry for trees and many other plants to grow. Instead, tough wild grasses take over the land. That is how these areas got the name *grasslands*.

Kangaroos have several different ways of staying cool in their harsh habitats. When they are hopping around quickly, they sweat. That helps them get rid of some body heat. When they stop hopping, they pant. Panting is when animals breathe quickly to bring in lots of fresh air to cool them down. They also may use their legs to dig the ground and lie on the cooler earth beneath.

Kangaroos sometimes lick their own arms to help keep them cool. As the moisture dries in the wind, it takes away some of the heat from their limbs.

What Do Kangaroos Eat?

Kangaroos are **herbivores**, which means they feed on mostly plants. Red and gray kangaroos are **grazers** that eat mainly green grass but they also will eat tough, spiny grasses and the leaves of other **bush** plants. The smaller **species** of kangaroo tend to eat leaves, shoots, and twigs. The musky rat kangaroo is different because it is the only kangaroo that eats some meat as well, usually in the form of insects or worms.

How do kangaroos eat?

When red and gray kangaroos eat grass, they crawl slowly along on all fours, munching as they go. They rest their tails and front paws on the ground and swing their back legs forward to move along. They can use their front paws to push aside shrubs to get at green grass.

Kangaroo mobs spend a lot of time eating. Depending on the season and the amount of food available, they spend between seven and fourteen hours every day eating.

Is grass hard to eat?

The kangaroo's stomach is designed for **digesting** tough, chewy grasses. Like cows, kangaroos chew the cud. First they chew and swallow the grass, which goes into one part of the stomach. Later they regurgitate it, which brings it back into the throat, and chew it again to make it soft enough to digest. Then they swallow this chewed cud, and it goes into a different part of the stomach for the final stage of digestion.

Where do kangaroos get water?

Like all animals, kangaroos need water to live. They get most of their water from the leafy plants that they eat, because these contain a lot of water. They also drink from pools or **watering holes** if they find one. If it is very dry, kangaroos may dig pits up to 3 feet (1 meter) deep to find water.

Kangaroos have very large front teeth for cropping and cutting. The large, flat molars farther back in their mouths help grind up their food.

Red and gray kangaroos usually **mate** in the spring or summer. The mother kangaroo gives birth to one **joey** at a time, around a month after mating. The tiny newborn kangaroo then spends between six and eleven months mostly inside its mother's pouch. The father and the rest of the mob help care for the joey when it comes out of the pouch.

This female kangaroo is ready to give birth. She has licked the pouch clean and created a path in her fur to show the baby the way to the pouch.

Can one mother have two joeys?

Female kangaroos are able to have two joeys developing at the same time. As soon as one baby is born and enters her pouch, the female is able to mate again. The second baby stays inside her body, waiting to be born until after the baby in the pouch leaves.

15

How do baby kangaroos get into the pouch?

When a kangaroo baby is first born, it is tiny. It is only 2.5 centimeters long and weighs less than 0.04 ounce (1 gram). It is about the size of a small jellybean and looks nothing like its parents. A newborn kangaroo is completely helpless. It has no hair to keep it warm, and it cannot hear or see. The only things on its little body that have developed are its nose, mouth, and tiny arms.

The newborn kangaroo uses its arms to crawl into its mother's pouch as soon as it has been born. Although it does not have far to go—only about 5 inches (12 centimeters)—this is a dangerous journey. If the baby **joey** takes too long, the heat of the sun may kill it, or it may die of exhaustion.

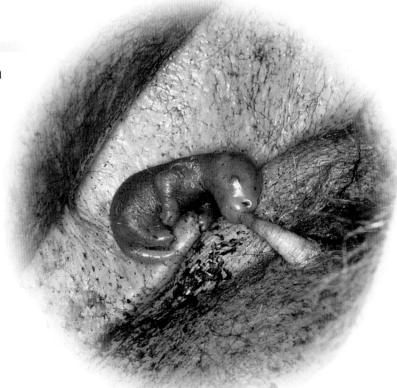

This newly born kangaroo is inside its mother's pouch. It found its way by smelling the trail its mother licked for it.

What happens inside the pouch?

As soon as it is safely inside the pouch, the baby joey chooses one of the four teats there to **suckle**. As it takes the teat in its mouth, the teat swells up and fills its mouth so the baby stays there and cannot fall off. The joey suckles almost non-stop inside the pouch for up to three or four months. The mother's milk helps the baby grow and develop. It grows larger and develops legs, ears, eyes, teeth, and hair.

What is suckling?

All **mammal** babies suckle. They drink milk from their mother's body. Mammal milk is a complete food for babies in the first part of their life, and it even provides all the water they need.

This joey is several months old. It has grown a lot since it arrived in the pouch, but it still needs to suckle for most of its food.

How does a pouch work?

Female kangaroos have muscles that control the pouch. They can close the pouch tight to keep a joey safe inside. If a mother wants the joey to leave, she makes the pouch go floppy and tips the baby out!

When does the joey leave the pouch?

At three or four months old, the **joey** pokes its head out of the pouch and starts to learn about life in the mob. A month or so later, it comes out every day to explore. By watching the other kangaroos, joeys learn skills such as where to find food and how to watch out for danger. By ten months old, most joeys have left the pouch, although they still stick their head in to suckle until they are a year or more old. By two or three, they are adults and can have young themselves.

Up to about a year old, joeys still dive headfirst into their mother's pouch for safety or comfort, until she pushes them out again!

How Do Kangaroos Relax?

Kangaroos spend the hottest times of the day resting, dozing, and chewing the cud. While they are relaxing together like this, members of a mob touch, sniff, and **groom** each other. Grooming is when one kangaroo uses its front paws to pick out dead skin, dirt, and tiny insect pests such as fleas from another's hair to keep it clean. Mother's groom young by licking them and using special grooming claws on their front paws.

Grooming and the mob

Grooming is an important part of a kangaroo mob's **social** life. When animals in a group groom, they end up smelling alike because of the scent in their saliva, or spit. It also is a friendly thing to do and makes the animals feel closer to each other. This helps the kangaroos in a mob feel more like a team.

When some kangaroos doze, others in a mob keep a look out for danger.

19

Playtime

Young kangaroos spend much of their relaxation time playing. **Joeys** play-fight first with mothers. They return from exploring and before they dive back into the pouch, they bump her head and get her to play-fight. Later, joeys play-fight together. When one joey wants to play-fight with another, it stands in front of its friend, scratching its sides as if showing off its **muscular** arms.

When joeys play-fight, they grab each other around the neck, touch front paws, and kick each other with their back legs. The end of a play-fight is when one pushes another over.

Why do joeys play?

Joeys play for the same reason that young animals all over the world play —for fun. Play also helps young kangaroos get to know the other members of the mob and their place within the group. Play—fighting also helps young **males** to learn good fighting skills because they might need these for real when they are older.

Do Kangaroos Talk to Each Other?

Kangaroo mobs use sounds to **communicate**—to tell each other things. For example, coughs can be a signal from one **male** to tell another he knows it is more **dominant**. Kangaroo mothers make clicking or clucking noises to call their joeys to them. When a kangaroo senses danger, it warns others in the mob by thumping its feet on the ground.

When members of a mob hear a kangaroo make a warning thump with its large back feet, they know it has spotted an enemy.

Kangaroos can twist their ears around to catch the sound of approaching danger or a warning thump from any direction.

21

Do Kangaroos from the Same Mob Fight?

Kangaroos in a mob may argue and push each other over various things such as food or shade, but these disagreements rarely result in real fights. Real fights happen when young **males** challenge the old **boomer** in a mob to try to win the right to **mate** with a **female**.

How does a fight start?

Most challenges begin when one male kangaroo threatens another with movements called **displays.** For example, a young male might stand upright and walk towards the other or pull on grass nearby. The old boomer will stand and puff out his chest in reply. Usually these threats are enough to make the weaker kangaroo realize that he would lose a real fight, and he turns and leaves.

The younger male kangaroo in this picture is showing the larger male that he wants to back down from the fight. Old males are so big that young males do not really stand a chance of beating them.

How big can a kangaroo get?

Most animals, including humans, stop growing when they become adults. Male red and gray kangaroos keep growing taller and stronger throughout their whole lives. Their front arms get bigger and more **muscular**, too. Even though the rate of growth slows as they get older, an old male can be more than half as big again as a young adult male.

How do kangaroos fight?

If an old boomer cannot scare off a young challenger, the two will fight. Real fighting is different from play-fighting. Kangaroos try to injure each other by kicking hard in each other's face and stomach using strong legs and sharp claws, and by biting ears. These fights are rare, and most are so one-sided that they end soon after they have begun.

Kangaroos use their front feet to hold their opponent while resting on their tail and giving mighty kicks with their huge and powerful back feet. Adult males often have thicker belly skin that helps protect them.

Does a Mob Ever Change?

Mobs of kangaroos change almost every year. A **boomer** is only the **dominant** member of a mob for about a year. It takes a **male** kangaroo about ten years to grow big and strong enough to win his place as leader. Then he only gets to remain dominant for a short time, because soon someone else wants a turn. When a stronger male challenges the leader to a fight and wins, he becomes the new leader of the mob.

When a dominant male kangaroo has to fight over who leads the mob, he may get badly injured. Old boomers that lose fights against stronger, younger males often die. If they survive, they have to leave the mob and go off to live alone. Most do not survive for very long alone.

Do young kangaroos stay in their mobs?

Most **female** kangaroos stay in the mob they were born in, at least for the first couple of years of life. Females develop strong bonds with their mothers. Young males usually leave the mob they were born in when new **joeys** are born. These young males often join together and form new mobs with females from other groups.

What happens when leaders die?

The mob also changes if important kangaroos die or get sick. Some die because of bad weather, such as when there is flooding or **drought**. Some die in **bush** fires— fires that spread quickly through the dry plants in summer. If older females or dominant males die, other mob members have to fight over which one should take over these important roles.

Drought is when an area of land has little or no rain for a long time. Without water, plants on the land dry up and die. Without plants, kangaroos may starve to death.

What Dangers Does a Mob Face?

There are few animal **predators** that can catch and eat large red and gray kangaroos, but there are several that hunt smaller kinds of kangaroos. These include the dingo, a kind of wild dog that lives in Australia, and the wedge-tailed eagle, which attacks **joeys**. In places where houses have been built near wild areas, pet cats and dogs may kill the smaller kangaroos.

Who watches out for danger?

One big advantage of living in a mob is that kangaroos can watch out for each other. They can take turns looking out for danger. When one bangs out a warning with its tail and hops away, the whole mob knows to scatter because danger is near.

This dingo is stalking kangaroos. Big kangaroos will fight off a dingo by kicking if they spot one coming.

Kangaroos and people

Many Australian farmers and landowners think of kangaroos as pests. They hunt or poison kangaroos to get rid of them. They say that red and gray kangaroos jump over fences onto farmland and eat plants meant for their sheep. But some people say that the kangaroos eat different grasses that sheep do not eat.

On the road

Members of many kangaroo mobs are knocked down by cars and trucks when they hop quickly across roads. Red and gray kangaroos are very heavy, so if a car hits one, both the animal and the people in the car may be seriously injured. Many people who live in the Australian **outback** have a metal grid on the front of their cars in case they collide with a kangaroo. These are called kangaroo bars.

Road warning signs like this one tell drivers where kangaroos might cross. These signs are intended to protect drivers as well as the kangaroos.

What is culling?

In some parts of Australia there are laws that stop people from hunting kangaroo mobs. In other areas, people are allowed to shoot a certain number of red and gray kangaroos in order to reduce their numbers. This is called culling. The skin and meat of the animals that are shot are sold. The leathery skins are used to make things such as shoes or soccer balls, and the meat is sold for people to eat or to be turned into pet food.

Kangaroos in danger

There are around two million red and gray kangaroos alive today. The **species** is not in danger. However, some of the smaller species of kangaroo, such as the hare wallabies, are **endangered**. They are in danger of becoming **extinct** because people are taking over the the kangaroo's **habitat** for buildings or farms. Some **conservation** organizations are working towards protecting these endangered species.

This is a prosperine rock wallaby, a member of an endangered kangaroo species.

Kangaroo Facts

How did kangaroos get their name?

One story that tells how kangaroos got their name says that when the first European explorers saw kangaroos in Australia, they asked the **Aborigines** what these strange creatures were called. The Aborigines replied, "Kangaroo," which means "I do not understand your question." But the explorers thought that was the animal's name!

Lifespan

In wildlife parks or zoos, kangaroos may reach twenty years old, but in the wild, most only live for six to eight years. This is because they face many dangers in the wild. Only about half of all **joeys** reach two years of age.

Forward only

The kangaroo's tail is very useful to help it balance when it is hopping, but it is so long and heavy that it makes walking forward slow and walking backward impossible!

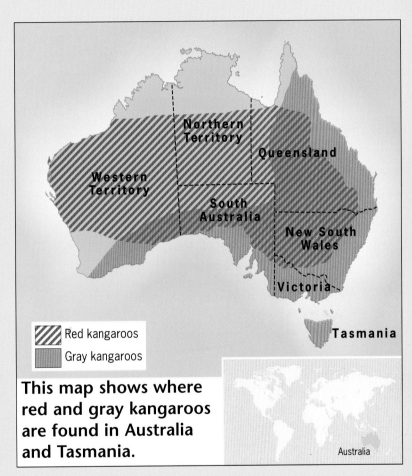

Red kangaroos
Gray kangaroos

This map shows where red and gray kangaroos are found in Australia and Tasmania.

Australia

Can kangaroos swim?

Kangaroos can swim quite well by doing a sort of doggy paddle. When they swim, they use their powerful legs and swing their tail from side to side.

Glossary

Aborigine   native Australian. They have lived in Australia for around 40,000 to 60,000 years.

boomer   large male kangaroo

bush   scrubland in Australia

communicate   pass on information

conservation   action to stop wild animals, plants, and places from dying out or being destroyed

desert   extremely hot and dry place with little rain

digest   what an animal's body does to break down its food and take out what it needs to live and grow

display   put on a show of actions or movements that sends a message to another animal

dominant   leader of a group or most important member

drought   when an area of land has little or no rain and the plants there dry up and die

endangered   when an animal or plant species is in danger of dying out

extinct   when a species has died out and no longer exists

female   animal that, when grown up, can become a mother

flyer   female kangaroo

grassland   area of land that is mainly covered in grass

grazer   animal that eats growing grass

groom   when one animal cleans bits of dirt, dead skin, or insect pests from the hair of another animal

habitat   where an animal or group of animals live

herbivore   animal that eats only or mainly plants and plant parts

home range   area within a habitat that a group of animals lives in

joey   young kangaroo

male   animal that, when grown up, can become a father

mammal   one of a group of animals that includes humans. All mammals feed their babies milk from their own bodies and have some hair.

marsupial   animal whose babies are carried in a pouch at the front of the mother's body

mate/mating   produce young. After a male and female kangaroo have mated, a baby begins to grow inside the female.

molar   flat-topped back tooth

muscular   full of muscles. Muscles are parts of the body that help to make the bones and the rest of the body move.

outback   wild Australian countryside, far from towns

predator   animal that hunts or catches other animals to eat

scrubland   area with sandy soil that has patches of trees and lots of slow-growing shrubs

social   live in a group

species   group of living things that are similar and can produce healthy offspring together

suckle   when a baby mammal drinks milk from its mother's body

watering hole   standing pool of water where animals go to drink

More Books to Read

Lantier-Sampon, Patricia and Judith Logan Lehne. *The Wonder of Kangaroos*. Milwaukee: Gareth Stevens, Inc., 2001.

Miller, Chuck. *Tree Kangaroos*. Chicago: Raintree, 2002.

Noonan, Diana. *The Kangaroo*. Broomall, Penn.: Chelsea House Publishers, 2003.

Penny. Malcolm. *Kangaroos*. Chicago: Raintree, 2003.

Stone, Tanya Lee. *Kangaroos*. Farmington Hills, Mich.: Gale Group, 2003.

Index